LOST AND FOUND

ALSO BY PETER ROBINSON

Poetry

The Benefit Forms
Going Out to Vote
A Part of Rosemary Laxton
Overdrawn Account
Anaglypta
This Other Life
More About the Weather
Entertaining Fates
Leaf-viewing

Translations

Six Poems by Ungaretti
The Disease of the Elm and other poems by Vittorio Sereni
Selected Poems of Vittorio Sereni
When I Was at my Most Beautiful and other poems 1953-1982
      by Noriko Ibaragi

Criticism

In the Circumstances: about Poems and Poets

Editor

With All the Views: Collected Poems of Adrian Stokes
Geoffrey Hill: Essays on his Work
Liverpool Accents: Seven Poets and a City

Peter Robinson

LOST AND FOUND

CARCANET

First published in 1997 by
Carcanet Press Limited
4th Floor, Conavon Court
12-16 Blackfriars Street
Manchester M3 5BA

A CIP catalogue record for this book
is available from the British Library
ISBN 1 85754 176 6

The publisher acknowledges financial assistance
from the Arts Council of England

Set in 10 pt Sabon by Bryan Williamson, Frome
Printed and bound in England by SRP Ltd, Exeter

ACKNOWLEDGEMENTS

I am grateful to the editors of the following publications where most of these poems or their earlier versions first appeared: *Ariel, English, The Independent, London Quarterly, Metre, Oxford Poetry, PN Review, Poetry Durham, Poetry Kanto, Poetry Wales, Prairie Schooner, Printed Matter, Scripsi, The Southern Review, Stand Magazine, The Swansea Review, Tabla, Thumbscrew* and *The Times Literary Supplement*.

'Leaf-viewing' was included in *The Poetry Book Society Anthology 1990*. 'Deep North' was also published in *Enlightened Groves: Essays in Honour of Professor Zenzo Suzuki* (Shohakusha, 1996). 'Lost Objects', 'Leaving Sapporo' and 'The Albert Dock' were anthologized in *Liverpool Accents: Seven Poets and a City* (Liverpool University Press, 1996). 'A Difficult Winter' appeared in the memorial volume, Dylan Francis: *The Risk of Being Alive: Writings on Medicine, Poetry, and Landscape* (Cambridge Quarterly Publications, 1996).

Some of these poems were first printed in *Leaf-viewing*, a limited edition published by Robert Jones in 1992. A few were broadcast in February 1994 with an interview recorded by Tim Dee for BBC Radio 3.

I would also like to thank Hiroshi Ozawa for his help in gaining permission to reproduce on the cover a detail from 'A Road (in the Suburbs of Paris)' by Rinjiro Hasegawa.

CONTENTS

One

A DEDICATION

In this quiet district, Shugakuin,
that rustling by the kitchen was
a tomcat I'd been warned of at my rubbish?

No, a large black crow with mocking caw
flaps to my neighbour's roofline
undaunted as I'm opening the back door.

Not samurai helmets in a river park, no,
they're firemen's and, from Kitayama dori, fireflies
darting on the hillside are headlamps of cars.

So I approach to distance as you hear
in the telephone's echo and delay.
Misunderstandings overlap, blur; things interfere.

O far interlocutor of my partial care,
for the long moments into silence now I say
words of explanation and launch them on the air.

EARLY DAYS

'...the past becomes dreamy because
its symbols have all vanished, and
the present too is dreamy because
it is linked with no memories.'
George Eliot

Mino City, not far from the airport;
its neon flickers on in daylight.

A dreamy childhood's freshly painted
pale spring colours on clean-stippled walls.

Sunday morning muffles all disturbance.
A pheasant goes stalking the aliens' garden.

It climbs grassed-over mounds, bypasses
puddled patches near white parked cars.

The afternoon is dreamy too. Osaka shimmers
through fluttering laundry on high terraces.

Into the dusk a bamboo wood murmurs.
It smudges, makes a bow to newcomers –

threatening or hardening who we can't but be.

THE RAINY SEASON

Low cloud in the best days for fireflies
forms a lid above blue roof-tiles.
Armories of trickling, bright umbrellas
guard entrance halls and café tills.

Close features turning in full buses
have a nervous calm, politeness;
and isolation brings home further losses,
also distance in unrecognising eyes.

This is the life of double space:
for some you seem too visible,
an eyesore on the crowd's pure surface;
for others, you're not there at all.

THINGS PAST

Their forty-seven casts were pocked and crumbling.
Showcases held dusty armour,
combs, gloves, someone's foot-warmer
and pictures of the night assault, snow tumbling
over a noble's disembodied head.

On ranks of neat grey stones it rained
and there a cold wind gusted.
Under an umbrella someone stooped to place more incense.
I saw a girl gaze from the windows
of her high-rise overlooking
the forty-seven tombs; persistent downpour
cut through aromatic smoke
pluming from the dampened
latest smoulderings of remembrance.

IN THE BORROWED SCENERY

1
Beneath a night of stars, the raucous
rice field with its fresh shoots starting
from dark calm, that shiny surface
gave back wooded hills, deep sky.
Being introduced to semblances
of elsewheres with their pains intact
brought from the borrowed scene false senses.
Its mountain echoed to a hoarse frog chorus.

2
At the fried food restaurant counter,
her father's phrase translated,
'Everything changed so quickly,' she had said.
It meant from malnutrition, sores,
the swollen bellies of first post-war years.
But her sense I had misunderstood
imagining friendship, my well-being.
Everything changed so quickly, to the good.

LEAF-VIEWING

Autumn's end, this was the season
for some looking back and forward.

Elsewhere old régimes were falling.
Party men and presidents fled.

Open thoughts, fresh feelings, fruit
and veg., consumer durables

some wanted: coal trains setting out
might reach their destination...

In aid of what the others wanted
certain streets were dragged with blood.

Among part-intelligible signs I'd stood
deciphering brands and, was it?, *murder*.

As the *walk – don't walk* light changed
still a Chinese demonstration,

vociferous, under escort, came on,
merged with forward swarming crowds

of Sunday shoppers in Shibuya:
'You a student?' 'No, a teacher.'

'Many teachers died there too.'
Words of peaceful intermingling

had re-echoed through the year:
you've lived in interesting times.

Across a wintry hemisphere
our separated fates converge.

Seasonal differences each endures,
each slight thaw and freeze.

There were pieces of misfortune
painted red still clinging to the trees.

1989

AT NEW YEAR

1
Fumiko, it was your idea
to take an early morning stroll
between the yacht marina pier
and trading harbour mole.

A coaster lay off in the tide.
From behind low cloud a clear
rose-pink disc, the new decade,
had started to appear.

On Tsu beach a driftwood fire
drew watchers of the trickling gore
which made old aspirations stir,
dyed waves that lapped the shore –

world pasts, each unstaunched nation,
bathed clean should no familiar
shadow on this swelling ocean
flood in with the year.

2
Last letters, a spattered uniform,
smoke-plumed aerial photographs
fill the military's ambivalent museum
at Yasukuni; epitaphs,

emblems from the dream of empire,
uniqueness, hating foreigners, fear
of weakness, suchlike did inspire
that *'brave, but is it necessary'*
dying for a moribund idea.

3
Feet stretched under a kotatsu
your minute Christian grandma
nearly fifty years a widow
slept on her tatami.

Half a life she's kept his shrine
in the provincial seaside home.
It had reminded me of mine.
Here, I am made welcome.

AN UNDETERMINED HEART

A fitted mat of leaves across the garden,
some laundry hung out on the line for ever,
this was the house he'd invited me to choose,
spacious, deserted, where alone a widow died.

The boarded-up windows lent oppressiveness
to shady corners of a bare room's tokonoma,
not a stick of furniture, the few amenities...
When he asked me did I like it I said, 'No.'

Like an empty vicarage before we had moved in
traces of displacement scuffed on walls and floor,
the scratches in a wooden step from its entry well
enough to remind me of that loneliness once more...

'Put away the personal sensations,' he had said,
'Such a loneliness we Japanese all wish to find.'
Called upon to move again I felt confused and sad.
'Your heart,' he added then, 'should be determined.'

I listened to the crows' advice, making up my mind.

THE COLD

Somewhere over Sakhalin –
or with what was Port Arthur below,
a pellucid azure on the wingline
glinting above wastes of snow,
there came her wrinkled pallor
on an in-flight world news interview
and a hat of grey rabbit fur
quivered as an east wind blew.

When hand and microphone appeared
she'd just come from a polling station,
and through the poor headset I heard
a voice-over translation.
'They promised us the future,'
she said of a lifetime missed,
'for seventy-odd years, but the future
I know now doesn't exist.'

She turned away and left behind
a creak of trodden ice.
'You found your work,' said the wind,
'on this or that ideological base –
but might guess from a Russian
rabbit-fur hat, her old
woman's face and disillusion,
underneath runs the cold.'

AS WE FOUND IT

'Die Welt des Glücklichen ist
eine andere als die des Unglücklichen.'
Ludwig Wittgenstein

'A fool sees not the same tree
that a wise man sees.'
William Blake

Large globules cradled on fat leaves,
uncertain sky, what might it be
clouds your vision, makes the days
a mass of petty irritation,
no more than the memories
or glimpses of some world not this?

The plants droop in humidity
as if, which ever way you look,
all we seem to do is fail –
a garden's plum and bamboo tree
skeined in sadness, love,
and you can't lift the veil.

Staring at loquat, maple, wistaria,
varieties I lump together as pine,
since you know the names of trees,
love, tell me if you can,
would this be the world
of the foolish or the happy,
the wise or the unhappy man?

You can't believe your eyes.
And when the changes come
bringing further unmapped fears,
being so bound up in ourselves
we barely notice them.

Near the Imperial Palace's
garden gate, we'd paused
to let thick traffic pass; I saw
a greying fringe blown forward
and the leaves, a gingko tree's,
flurrying about your forehead
tousled by the breeze.

What caused it? Whether the breeze,
your hair or gingko leaves
or else the whole ensemble
blowing together, my thought agrees,
suddenly fits its resemblance
and we seem content to be
a moment somewhere on the surface
of any world at peace.

LOST OBJECTS

A blue purse on a fire-escape!
In this country it's a custom.
Finding some lost property,
a ring, or this blue purse here,
considerately someone
will place it in full view nearby
on a wall, a window sill.

Everywhere you notice them
precariously balanced
on arm-rests of commuter trains
or a bridge's curving parapet,
some person's pocket book, a diary
– these mementos patiently
awaiting whose return?

Seen from tiered expressway lanes
or the shinkansen tracks,
misplaced items interrupt skylines.
It's Liberty with her torch upraised,
a Bavarian castle: love hotels
are something missing floated clear
of flats and close-packed houses.

As the rush-hour services clatter
through residential districts
on balconies washed sheets flutter,
whole conurbations of them;
in entryways, a clutter
of bikes, umbrellas, shoes has found
some means of coming home.

Leaving a local station platform
under white sky filled with heat,
a memory, loved one, or poem
has been left behind. But what?
Wordless in front of the next
lost property office's window
you find yourself looking perplexed.

REST YOUR EYES

Rest your eyes on the sodden greens
with thick grey crowding under
or the ones rice shoots remember
— a charm against resentment.

The lizard landed on a pane
sticking to its lighted surface
licks at a fly that came to wander,
but did not find contentment.

Tomorrow you will wake to nothing,
the nothing that knows you by sight.
Its early cloud is fleeced with sun.
Once more you must explain

for what is near is fading
and death will have your eyes
(the tea, bamboo leaves, mould receding)
perhaps before their body dies.

THE MONK'S GARDEN

My landlord, back straight,
sits quite still to contemplate
perfect raked gravel.

*

Ripples of its sea
undulate out fluently
to far-flung islands.

*

Arranged rocks conceal
from the persecution's zeal
a stepping-stone cross.

*

Lost grace fills the eyes;
rent unpaid, I realize
it's Easter Sunday.

ON DROPS OF RAIN

'el muerto no es un muerto: es la muerte.'
Jorges Luis Borges

Electric cables, telephone wires
strung between the dark wood houses,
over ground because of earthquakes,
and in June, the rainy season,
entranced, I'm watching droplets run
down a sagging power-line;
they slip off at its lowest point,
distinct, a continuous stream
of lives cut short by endless causes.
How each one glistens as it falls…

We do not mourn the ones dead poets mourned
– some words to that effect you wrote.
But in the glinting drops returned
dying generations, now our own.
You mourn yourself, are just another
of the ones the poets mourn:
a daughter, wife, a great friend, mother.
We don't mourn the ones dead poets mourned?

BACKGROUND NOISE

Silence, no, I like it too:
the snicker of an air-con,
perpetual dripping of a tap
or birdsong in the dawn.

Then others' voices come
whispering on telephones –
wrong numbers, friends, and some
imaginary ones...

You like to think you're gone
but here it is again,
a light tenor, wry head tone,
unmistakably your father's strain.

Years back, it grew stronger
as he shouted up the stairs –
nettled, raised in anger,
reacting to his fears...

Humming in the throat I hear, or
notice start behind a glance
thrown at some blind corner mirror,
his face, my silence.

A WELL-MADE CRISIS

1
On a first-floor corridor
much the worse for wear
there's a glass display case,
inside it, dusty plaster casts:
Winged Victory of Samothrace,
Laocoön, Venus, torsos, busts...

2
Below, the inner courtyard
of a four-square red brick building;
its gravel paths are overgrown.
Who walks there? No one is.
The pine trees have been cut back hard.
By card catalogue drawer-files, alone,
I find myself yielding
again to an awkward sensation
in the paintwork's psoriasis,
eczemas of damp and mould.

3
Among still gestures, meaning gone,
paint lifted from striated wood
of pale green window frame and door.
So fallen into disrepair
these jaded poor memorials,
what were they brought here for?
Europe, Greece, a dingy corner:
my mind was made up there.

A PLACE WORTH VISITING

'like the music of one's native tongue
heard in some far-off country'
William Hazlitt

On the tourist route through hell
there were huge, tame crows
landed from serpentine boughs
of pine trees arching low
above my guide's head and my own.
We passed the fresh mud flows
and holes where sulphur clouds rose
in gushing columns; I'd turn and go,
but, a guest, it seemed best to follow
with souvenir, rudimentary map, the charms
to keep me on this straight and narrow;
each indrawn breath a pungent smell
of laboratories, café smoke plumes,
or refined exhalations, car fumes
along the tourist route through hell.

On the tourist route through hell
my guide came out with something choice:
'I'm myself in hell,' he said, a smile,
a self-important grimness to his voice.
He asked me would I be able to write
a poem about this famous place
where pieces of naked video girl
were trampled in the detritus
of swerving wheels; I glimpsed her face
(feigned mask of anguish or delight)
and thought, 'Like hell you are: I might.'
His unhappiness; still, I couldn't tell
what family inferno he had hinted,
ageing, ill, or thing he wanted
from the tourist route through hell.

On the tourist route through hell,
'I felt I'd died and no one noticed,'
a sufferer from the alien's disease
complained of chances missed.
She'd blame it on the Japanese.
Ex-patriots, bought, compelled
to trade our culture or appease
the foreign devils...Had we a hope
in hell of finding some escape?
Under umbrellas, through steady drizzle
and tinkling van microphones
whose information voices puzzle,
I listened to the tune for going home:
a strain of Auld Lang Syne come
to the tourist route through hell.

A TRIBE OF MONKEYS

Over Mino waterfall,
its picnic sites and courting places,
out from shadowed undergrowth
along steep roadside slopes
on Christmas Day, last light declining,
a tribe of monkeys lopes.

One licks a broken bottle's lip;
one stares into a dead beer can;
this wounded one with forepaw crooked
scampers to its family group
where a breast-feeding one
pauses, looks, and turns
to groom her sucking baby's head.

Close, one screeches on a fence,
perhaps to warn them of the man
who, halted in the first dark, stands
amongst them, oddly drawn
towards their creaturely migration
that feeds on our absurd left-overs.

Married friends by parking spaces
and my wife wait patiently.
Why linger at this distance?
A motor cycle's sweeping ray
at full beam in the tunnel mouth
silhouettes us and is gone.

Though gripped by these peculiar
picnic-spot-scavenging scenes,
the truth is I can't stay.
Through a narrow mountain gap
Osaka stretches to grasp us,
new town walkways, slip-roads, signs
constellated on a blackness
leaping to absorb our hosts' white car.

COVERAGE

1

A stripe of light across mat floor,
a stray cat whines;
the sky's a wispy blue and one more
day of life begins
with glinting leaves; above the lines
of dragon-featured rooftiles
a sacred mountain's peaking.

2

Midnight, Greenwich mean time,
this voice is the BBC World Service
in calm accent speaking
news that I rose not to miss;
garden songbirds in the season's
unusual pre-spring mildness
freak with notes a chorus
of claim and counter-claim.

3

St Valentine, what reasons
of state will serve to cover
margins of tactical error
for which none dare apologize?
Despite an old year's resolutions,
just war, Jesus, whose eye sees
if we've become a polished mirror
of our enemies?

14 February 1991

MAPLE LEAF

Maple leaf shapes in the frosted pane,
my kitchen door gives on to nothing,
grey block wall and shrub of some kind,
maculate laurel, flustered by a wind.

The air's so cold snowfall remains
as white cowls on the leaves and boughs.
At dusk, I wonder would they care
to come inside, or stay outside.

Aortas, white flags, broken stars,
the leaves are anything you want
some think, an emblem of the firmament
and your body in it, maybe aching scars.

Such words have let you understand,
but they would throw the dictionary
then ask the likes of me to write
our long disgrace in other terms.

I can't. The fallen snow on branches
makes ghosts of years that flinch and reach,
and if we'd just invented them
they wouldn't mean a thing.

When sun breaks through the blank snow cloud
and garden cowls are loudly melting,
each maple leaf shape in the frosted pane
glows palely with a borrowed green.

Two

IN THE TWILIGHT

Although we have our doubts
about streaks of pinkish amber
clouds in an evening's mauve,
you're what I wouldn't be without:
a municipal crematorium
or small brick memorial,
as if you were the last of them
to have died or gone away.

In quandaries on traffic islands
out through Leiden's built-up fringes,
see opulent verges' intensified green
break up tarmac, have twinges
of what? Erotic memories,
light beer foam, road sign arrows,
a smell of close canals? Who knows
at the end of one more day.

Yet though it's said you are about
to leave or have just disappeared
we continue through a twilight
solid with changes: for example,
a heron by duckweed-still water
stealthily treads with sidling neck;
the corporation flats turn sombre;
a beak darts at its prey.

A JOURNEY IN SUMMER

i.m. Maria Teresa Sereni

1
High cold streams couldn't drown the hum
of traffic from an autostrada,
children's voices also, some
cries, excited tantrums, harder
phrases; then a remnant
of hurt in others' tendernesses
reached up to the balcony
with toilet built above a river,
and vast matrimonial bed...
which meant we could clearly still remember
though that September seemed so distant.

Even the Rienza didn't deafen
slurred words about unbroken sunshine
from Helga the servant girl scratching her knee
in a kitchen, Rosa her aunt descanting
to dance bands on the radio
– where I found a thing to say
as the poor girl meningitis had made silly
kept insisting on good weather though the sky was overcast,
with her eyes squeezed shut to remember
perhaps where Rome is, or Verona,
and if we were leaving the day we'd go
when September still seemed very far away.

2

A hubbub of late diners above the water's roar
caught us a moment, distracted from the note
of divorce and spoiling in abandoned properties
– which is why a hotel's cleaned façade,
lanterns, laid cloths in the open,
polished glass and steel above a bar
told how time made sanitized
would be the only antidote.

Still to know yourself and then know
who the others are...At Valleggio sul Mincio
my sister mentioned stones of this river
were impregnated with blood from Solferino;
even now when it rains a memory
of hurt will return as if we'd see
that what contentment time may offer
can't come of amnesia.

3

This was the room where work was done,
these the chairs and tables;
there on a wall was his photograph of Saba,
beret, pipe and stick quite visible;
and here above your gothic novels,
the painter's gift, a small Chagall.

Pigòt, your mother with such ostentation
managed the palaver of a tea ritual
while you, a buddha from the therapy,
enlightened, it seemed, by resignation,
spoke the careful English you knew well
but hadn't dare use with us before.

Then your mother would remember
her literary courtship, honeymoon in wartime,
a doll on the coverlet in a hotel room
and looked to you for confirmation –
a shadow of yourself, so quickly tired,
receiving us though in a hospital robe.

You can't go now there's too much to be done
and how unfair not to be here any more,
were the words recurring later...
when it struck me your father's books and papers
had been pushing us away from, not towards,
those lives we couldn't share.

4
'How unfair...' he was saying as we noticed
choked tears at the corners of his eyes
and a face just turned
away to mourn lives gone unmourned,
perhaps a mother and the other women lost
again as his phrase just died.

Then into a stopped conversation, her hand
reached for the crumpled shoulder a moment,
drawing it nearer to the sensed and thought
under canvas awnings in a dark back court
amongst chatter, and fresh orders, and
finished dishes of another restaurant.

5

Maybe later couples from the neighbouring farms
had made love in these ruins, scratched their names
on damp-stained plasterwork where bitter memories
for those who had survived through winters
round a single fire remained;
still, earthquake cracks presented no problem
to builders who could just unstitch
and stitch walls up again.

Cobwebs, charred beams, bits of straw
in the grate of a place where someone died
had us pondering events, eventualities;
she was saying we shouldn't be tied
to the past's requirements, these
thoughts of promise unfulfilled or
hopes become mere burdens when
finally we get to decide.

Then she pointed at a butterfly
trapped inside the car,
which might have arrived via emptied rooms
from a wall of the dead hard by.

6

Those women who had lost their way
back from a house we'd come to see
in a field of head-high sunflowers
became two disembodied voices
calling more directions to each other.

And to me intuiting where they'd gone
overhearing someone else's inspiration
it seemed the yellow heads would turn
to lead a straying soldier home
with storm clouds heaped above a barn
and words of your father's in translation
crossing the frontiers of nineteen-forty-one
emerged from that absence into which you were born.

7
'The cradle by St Ambrose holds
himself, not his child, and he's nothing to do
with the Banco Ambrosiano,'
so a monk smiled leading us through
his monastery's picture gallery
and straightening his face went on,
'but with a swarm of bees
that didn't sting the sleeping child
and with this saint's mellifluous tongue.'

There were hives stood near a ruined door
and one bee hit me at the ear
where it burned and stung –
and though my wife with tender suck
could remove the barb before
its poison had properly struck,
I was thinking: How unfair
to feel a thing you can hardly share
or be among the ones diseases choose.

NABUCCO

Then you let thought go
to an open night above front stage,
Babylonian towers about to crack
and a rustle from spectators quietening down
in the Arena at Verona, to the back
of a man turning round with a hiss
saying 'Via!' to a chatting foreigner
because perhaps he thought we couldn't hear
or wouldn't understand.

And you let thought go
to the forty children in a school
probably machine-gunned, the woman
with a baby in her arms evacuated
from a shelled walled city who stated
she didn't want to live any more
— while another ceasefire failed to hold,
cameras of the opinion-making world
picked across dead faces in a war zone,
peace emissaries were seen walking alone
as further calls for weapon shipments came
and someone somewhere else was to blame
for the horrors none could countermand.

So you let thought go
to the chorus of down-trodden ones
crowding towards their orchestra pit
at the final sustain of *Va pensiero*,
that anthem to a recoverable land,
when the entire audience call 'bis, bis'
because they want to hear it again
with yet more feeling and the smart man raises
his baton hand.

TO A VICAR'S DAUGHTER

Beside a white table cloth
the mirrored wall was doubling us both
in that afternoon café, our brief time
quickened from the facial pantomime,
as if by still waters when the tip of every leaf
reaches to touch its own reflection in self-disbelief.

Life hanging by a thread
of words, you'd thought that were you dead
you wouldn't mind: you had had enough
– but, forgive me, I was more disposed to laugh,
though you too had grown up in some chilly vicarage,
lost faith, likewise, had come of age
wrestling with the angel of what you might write, and
not found that your burden much lightened.

Still there's gratitude and hope
despite the time gone quickly; I can't stop
time, summer in St Martin's Lane, or bring
back the glitter of a beaten metal ear-ring
quivering on the polished café wall,
but may redouble it in memory if you recall
being awkwardly held for just a moment
between a slot of sky and crammed pavement.

THE YELLOW TANK

for Diethard and Waltraud Leopold

Only a yellow water tank
stained with rain smears and some rust
on a flat apartment roof –
it stares at you from room to room;
and far too near to have perspective,
you could think this yellow tank
a punch in the eye or personal affront
as it shifts above the breakfast table.

Glimpsed through dwarf palm fingers
on your balcony, the thing can seem
a beach resort accessory
or ready-made in an art museum:
its service ladder and overflow
have elegant hooks like croziers,
raised rabbits to imply a joke,
philosophers' scare-marks or sows' ears.

Not funny, a memory of sunlight
throughout the rainy season,
it penetrates our mist-filled mornings,
reconciles three elements;
I've seen it graced by cloudless nights,
full moons, and briefly perching crows;
against the hillside's heaving pines
the yellow tank is all repose.

Rather than melting snowy ranges,
nippled hills, golf nets, rooftiles,
afforestation, or glimpse of ocean,
maybe you prefer this tank;
as with a disaffected child,
photograph, make fusses of it,
until the yellow water tank blesses,
answers us back with words.

LEAVING SAPPORO

for Teruhiko Nagao

This had not happened before.
You'd stopped your car askew outside the airport.
Running to the check-in desk I caught
a girl's polite-voiced information:
'I'm sorry; I'm afraid, sir, this flight has gone.'
And turning, at a loss, I saw
the tailplane taxi from its boarding gate.

Then the feeling of falling back into a place
with labels, lounges, luggage carousels
had baffled and arrested me,
the projects, a whole day's purpose dissipating
to a huddle of executives wreathed in smoke.
Outbound flight-lists; merely waiting,
I was too disaffected to view the famous lake,
as if life itself had gone on stand-by
and there'd be no escape to make.

But all morning you were standing by.
Daylight thickened on the café window pane.
A sheaf of tickets in my hand, I'd try
this or that flight, destination or airline,
anything, it seemed, to get into the sky
and, failing, noticed *Welcome to Hokkaido*
once again; and when we met again
you'd be working on your sense of shame.
Although I said it didn't much matter
whether I reached home sooner or later
you said you'd always hold yourself to blame.

Blame the unfinished expressway spur,
polythene flounces on its elevated sections,
the sculpture of its stanchions petrified from cloud;
or blame that Monday morning traffic
with queues as when a lorry's shed its load;
blame a continuous drizzling rain
which taunted squeaky windscreen wipers
down an approach road's outer lane;
blame the unforeseen through which we live,
this intimate running up against a sullen sky
and chance encounter with a city fringe's detail
– but, yourself, forgive.

THE VIEWS FROM A BRIDGE

The wish to die or murder someone,
fear of heights, that recurrent dream when
you're falling, falling from a parapet's edge
— I'm reminded of them each day at the bridge
by my slight vertigo.

Yet glancing once into the river ravine
past outcrops of strata and foliage, I'd been
gripped by tints of picnickers on rocks between
cliffs and the water below.

Or that pellucid day in earliest spring,
I watched the tip feathers of a hawk's wing
twitch to adjust fresh swooping and circling
above the traffic flow.

Skyline of the misty city loosening to distance,
there curved above my head the steel grille fence;
some votive chrysanthemums and a saké pot
remained near a tablet beside the sheer drop:
this is where suicides go.

Today, when ochres, umbers, russets, crimsons,
ripe orange, yellow, rust, almost maroons
of leaves had made a plenitude, police
stopped and climbed to see how someone else
had not found it so.

BUS STOPS

1

Lit route numbers approach through the dusk.
Another day's sunset closes to black.
Buses pass like the latest of our lost possibilities.
Did I think that the world would exist
if we stood at a distance and smiled?
Yet even as you dream it's going past,
perhaps the last comes glimmering uphill
carrying with it whatever life promised
on its journey across the suicides' bridge
then up between fairground and zoo
– for all the while it's dreaming you,
a dubious newcomer, foreign
guestworker at a bus stop who'd ask,
'Is this the right dark to be travelling home in?'

2

At the one where we get off, below
a latticework of steel struts,
crows are flitting about the glow
like great black moths in candlelight.
Its illuminated bands are purple, red and white;
they tint the night's mist
a violet colour in chilly days
toward the year's and the century's end,
and you stare at that luminous haze
round our north-eastern broadcasting tower
as if it were the messages they send
picturing to others how we are.

CURRICULUM VITAE

for Rosemary Laxton

It was just like another lost picture of mine.
You were typing reports, about ready to go,
with face in profile and frozen snow
along spiked, lifting branches of the pine.

Over twenty years back, looking into a brown
exercise book you'd use for recipes,
'Our end is Life. Put out to sea'
I found MacNeice's poem copied down.

The hospice, admission ward, listed care
for others, violence, a lack of love…
'Our end is Life' but you don't have
to put to sea, as it is what you are.

Three

THEIR FEARS

1

A week of early waking: jet lag and birdsong
welcome in the dawn; then first Tube trains
shudder through these house foundations
and bed frame, mattress, to my stomach.
They start a trembling, hunger or desire
in the emptiness, this want of breakfast
or compulsion to undergo some further test
like a slip-glazed pot offered up to the fire.

2

Before her is a fenced forest with a gate
and sign saying *Keep Out: Private.*
She enters, somehow understands.
Laughing head flung back, she knows
his fear of even getting close
and need to appear not to have any needs,
has foreseen it, the hollowed-out fate
of the man with his hair in her hands.

THE HAPPINESS PLANT

There was a mist on the marshalling yards;
a yucca, the happiness plant,
its top sealed with a red solution,
had forced up arms, like Daphne's, at its sides;
the bathroom window had been somehow broken
as if in a struggle or fit of rage
and a yellowed lace curtain, drawn across it,
tried to make light of the jagged shards.

This perishable matter would stay and rot for years
as if to test belief in the power of his fridge
where everything forever may be preserved,
though somebody's gone off with what was legally hers,
and an end game's pieces stood waiting for the end
on an ironing board with a hole burnt in its cloth:
yet what if the opponent would not understand
that the effort itself had taken all our breath?

Outside, incessant noises from machinery and cars
framed the silence of this lofty room
where dusty book jackets, soft toys, what was
the memory of another, outlive the afternoon.
Here pages of a barely to be finished novel lie
variously in sheafs of a latest draft.
Love's failures are carried on and on in other words
and the writing problems have been talked to death.

Across unemptied ashtrays and the minute pause
between clicks on an answerphone, there rises
the wish to avoid being drawn, just suppose,
into another of so many lost causes,
for there is a mist on the marshalling yards
and though a yucca, the happiness plant,
its top sealed with a red solution,
has forced up arms, like Daphne's, at its sides,
the burden of the air still refuses to lift.

RED WEDNESDAY

The roads are empty this mid-morning.
Only an occasional car goes by.
I'd left you to arrange your things
and am puzzled why
tomorrow or the next night you will sleep
amongst them and awake alone
in a borrowed flat above a shop,
mournful now I'm gone.

Anyway, beyond Barnes railway bridge
where the river tends, I stroll along
and keep my station without courage
enough to say it's wrong
that objects which were ours to have
anyone should be asked to lose.
There's something missing from our love
that won't come back, God knows.

It's as if the Muse had gone to pack
with tired eyes, uncertain eyes,
but a firm determined look,
and left me in a daze
where election posters are Lib-Dem
on set-back houses, or they're Conservative.
We'd outlined what we want, like them,
not what we have to give.

At Hammersmith, pubs offer discount beer.
Papershops announce a Labour lead.
Though hopes for change would disappear
I can sense a need
to hold in mind each cherished feature
from the years we had laid waste,
and even for the sake of some lost future
keep faith with that past.

Hyde Park at dusk, the Serpentine;
here above a tower block now
pink clouds form a fragile line
in thickening blue,
and Queensway has more premises for sale.
Passing haunts in business still, I find
signs we'd recognize only too well
though someone's left behind.

Today's stock market prices tumbled.
We might have been already in the red.
Our securities had crumbled.
Am I represented
by a mandarin duck's slight wake,
or father attempting to launch his son's kite,
or lovers on a bench who embrace as I walk
past them into twilight?

1 April 1992

PENALTIES

for Mark Ford

After a bathroom's turquoise roof
with its dragon tails of mould,
a black look or blank look, on the whole
it might be time to make my move.

The tokonoma makes a handy goal.
You flick a miniature world cup football
off the tatami, against a flimsy wall,
to volley it past my splaying hands.

What do I do? Dive left or right
and imagine I'm choosing how to live
or taking, before it's too late,
another false alternative?

Bad luck. The language won't improve.
Better not sacrifice a love
for however many words, you say.
But do we even have the choice?

Whatever I'd been looking for –
whether a 'both…and', an 'either…or'
or, putting it mildly, none of the above,
it's as if you'd implied life itself were

not an invitation to another goal-less draw.

NOSTALGIA FOR THE PRESENT

In a cliff-face lake front frame,
pink and ochre with grey pilasters
and oval-topped windows,
a dainty hydro-electric plant
built in the early century seems
such a thing as appears in dreams
of deserted piazzas with distant trains.

A statue in white wind-ruffled stone
with an abstract name like Melancholy
is forgotten by locals, ignored by those
emerging from the porticoes
at sunset: somebody, let's say,
whose elongated shadow ends
where a rock wall meets a lawn,
one of a child's imaginary friends
invented, cherished to fend off
the empty hours, or lack of love;
and walking with me by the shore,
he suspects we might be more
accepting of the architecture.

You see a lido's moulded concrete
landing-stage canopy, curved sheet glass,
and parked at angles on display,
two number-plate-less cars;
the restaurant terrace is curious
with eyes that glance at them and us,
you and I trying to recuperate
from a premature nostalgia
at the merely being here.

Young divers splash among the stakes
of a rickety pleasure boat pier.
Behind us, under cloudless blue,
there'd been undeniable urges.
We're staring in the dusk to see
if from moorings, beach names,
roadsigns and troubled grass verges,
would emerge a continuity.

So nothing more alarming than a topless torso,
the wild goose chase of whitening waves
across the lake as smoke wisps slide
from explosions of each firework
allows the moon, a whole orange now,
to move above black cypresses
by a swollen stone-pillared balustrade
and lovers' bronzed or brazen faces
swim this avenue.

THE ALBERT DOCK

for David Mather

Because of a derailment on the line
between this port and an old coal mining
town I lived in thirty years ago,
I waited an hour for you, not knowing
why it was you hadn't come
and contemplated going back home,
while a naval patrol boat and steam tug took
their turns to glide out through a lock
and into the Mersey estuary.

Playing at the Nineteenth Century
a Baptist Mission in fancy dress
singing hymns, with scripted speeches,
was to make the dull red sandstone
of converted warehouse dockland
chime once more with confidence;
but just now I couldn't see the sense,
and leaning on black stanchion chains
painted solid, asked what remains
from when this port was in its hey-day,
a pensioner gone past saying
over dark dock water, 'There's no fish here,'
to a seagull swooping on the psalm-filled air.

So when shops are discounting all their stock
and some haven't even a memory of work,
when a thin film of our past's what you get,
the city where we both grew is in debt
to Swiss banks and the Japanese,
you might notice through a gallery's
shielded window, elegantly framed,
a watery lithograph of the famous
river with its ferry, its far shore,
then a pizza parlour, a karaoke bar –
and none of it making much sense any more.

DEEP NORTH

'What silence
penetrating rock
the voice of the cicada'
Matsuo Bashō

On the platform at Sendai
waiting brought up this example:
were there one or more voices
in his cicada verses,
silence penetrating rock
at a local mountain temple?
'They're plural,' you'd reply.

And were close readers
of the English graveyard school
code-breakers redeployed
once hostilities had ended?
I wondered was it true,
your half-serious theory
that Bashō was a government spy?

Wood stakes at Yamadera
were memorials for their dead
with new names to fend off terror
at death, you might have said
staring at rice fields and roofshapes
from the highest viewing platform –
inspiration for a visiting poet.

But I would be obliged to wait,
let sound sink into stone.
A noise of gunfire, I supposed,
uncovered thoughts of someone
dead ten years, but no less hurt
at warfare and war's echoes.
It was just a birdscarer's report.

HEARING DIFFICULTIES

About the shell of my right ear
it's true there's something ominous.
Added to the chorus
                of voices I can hear
is a thin, continuous
rushing noise like the sound of the sea
or like an old valve record player
left on through the night.

*

In a hearing clinic's waiting room
someone's worse off than yourself;
putting up the CT scan
he shows what lies beneath the skin
and bad news after hours of patience
arrives in the shape
of a paler shape about the size of a coin.

*

'God help you' comes from overseas.
It means *the very best of luck*
in the English of a Japanese,
and it's true you need it when

a consultant pats you on the knee
offering some courage,
lays his hands on you and says,
'You'll be wondering soon: why me?'

*

But I was thinking: Well, why not?
What would they mean, the hours of boredom
and jokes about a poet going deaf,
all things being equal in sickness and in death,
if not that here's just another of those people?

So when you tell him we're getting a divorce
(letting him know as a matter of course)
he replies, 'It never rains but it pours.'

CLEARING THE WOOD

'Ma fui certo che il bosco
non è senza via d'uscita'
Mario Luzi

Replenishing a bonfire wants fronds from the copse,
Or stripping ivy out of strangled boughs
She cuts through twigs; replenishing allows
Embers glowing red hot to collapse.

Making the distance with coffee cups, I traipse
After hiss of sap and smoke that goes
Rising above her spinny now breeze blows:
Yesterdays marred by quarrelling or rapes.

Let me slip away without a sound
And live the rest: seed packets, coins, pub lunches,
Xmas decorations, overcast skies.

Tomorrow, white foxgloves will prick cleared ground
Or dappled shade, estate and grange surprise –
Never again these intertwining branches.

Four

SEVEN PHEASANTS

Seven pheasants adventured this far
into your city, along its river fringes

(despite threats from the hunter's gun),
are sign enough of life for me.

Strollers paused above a parapet see
their proud green necks held straight.

Eyes have bluish, white and red patches.
They stoop between grassblades to eat.

These ones beside the wall's foot run
at first hints of a danger we must be –

not meaning any harm, allowed the time –
late morning in our hiatus holiday.

We've been needing some heartfelt changes,
things accepted for what they are.

Take courage: along the river fringes
seven pheasants had ventured this far.

A DIFFICULT WINTER

i.m. Dylan Francis

When freezing fog fills the city streets
and pollution warnings have closed the roads,
when bad news comes to make me cry
by letter, or by telephone,
it seems there's little else to say
though a quiet voice keeps asking why
and we close the shutters on another day.

You're wondering what more could be done.
Another had thought it best to die
by his own hand, in bed, alone.
I hear from the friend who left a note
for this young man already gone:
you'd think that to be dead itself
criticized those who would go on.

Tracing the path across a field
covered in fog like a disease,
it's as if I were some curious child
picking out hoof prints, one who plays
while low hills re-emerge, a farm,
and every shrub half glimpsed is an event,
a memory's precise alarm.

The ambitions of youth had been confined;
without his help, they'd found a limit;
and the ghost you were about to meet
appearing from fog, the one detained,
one most burdened with promise,
it seemed he hadn't made it.
It was written all over my face.

LATE ROMAN FRAGMENT

for Marcus Perryman

Mist hung among the deciduous trees
in the Parco Ducale; mist had invaded
its lake and environs, filtered the distance
down avenues broad as parade grounds;
two gesturing men emerge by chance
at an oval of water with cruising swans
and flotillas of ducks, but they've little idea
what's lying below, what mysteries.

There's a toy train on its circular track
with the stations marked: Roma, Torino,
but closed for the winter; a mother and child
dawdle by benches near shut ice-cream stalls
– as if to keep going round and around
were the best he hoped for in this world
and, half revealed, an urge to comprehend
turns on itself in mid-January cold.

Remember the folly, a late Roman fragment
constructed in brick some two centuries ago,
and through the mist we find it now,
though where would be telling, as if it meant
some secret information, a burden you show
adopting the role of whoever, a Marlow,
or Ancient Mariner doomed to test
the patience of his saddened wedding guest.

Back to these sudden nebulous spaces,
pieces of somebody's parkland, preserved,
surviving in overrun, fume-polluted cities,
I come where we're able to breathe again;
it's like hearing a story from start to finish
but, remind me then, what were the good
of explaining, what was it you wanted,
if not just to be understood?

A CLASSICAL LANDSCAPE

The grass and trees forget –
they stand aloof, indifferent.
With difficulty I keep my balance
along the old path trouble knows
where daffodils waver beside a stream,
Baucis and Philemon have departed
or been altered to a pair of trees.
Now across these water meadows
(their boats below eye-level)
the standing tourists glide;
sheep are cropping; cattle graze
beneath that Corinthian pile
of the art museum; cyclists ride
down paths which people once known had taken
while others, unfulfilled, died.

So these scenes have been sublimed
to a stretch of landscaped garden,
figures sketched by another hand –
much sharper, simplified under skies
where talk that passed expressed a sorry
view of twenty years.
                              Watery eyes
watch these figures stroll under trees
or gaze ahead from convenient benches
at hope's perspectives in time become regret,
at weeping branches and necessary loss.
Though peace had been declared between us
there came no triumph or relief.
Some shrubs were breaking into blossom;
willows eased into leaf.

BEFORE AN OPERATION

Because it seems the worst is just to wait
and also for this you once endured
his poor desires, until he'd had enough,
becoming yourself, my only lost love,
despite the outward appearances
days themselves had weighed on us.

Now knowing how in another time
I'd have slowly died without a chance,
the rest of life comes as this bonus.
I glimpse a swallow's dip and climb
through aerials, the chimney pots,
in a square of blue where a single star
glinted above semi-circular rooftiles
not more than a couple of nights ago.

I catch a blackbird's song this spring
and, late, young people's voices rise
from a cleft of the street below,
yet today in a freshening breeze
a wooden shutter would suddenly swing
and across the sickbed where I'm lying
cast its intricate shadow.

A BURNING HEAD

1

These leaves had caught the eye
in backwaters of days
at waiting's end, but why
does the breeze take such huge liberties?

How could it have been
our notorious east wind,
the ghost of Joe Stalin,
had carried pain away?

Sibilant, it came funnelling
through hospital high-rise,
a torment to trees
beside a children's playground

– which follows me everywhere!
And what are tender branches
but an invitation
to someone coming round?

2

Through blurred faces by the bed
hovering as I roll and twist
tubes leading from the nose,
spine, penis, and both wrists –
'What day is it? What year?
Where are you?' somebody insists.

Reeling them off the top of my head
like a clever schoolboy's homework shows
I'm with it, I'm not gone, I'm still here!

3

Then this is how I picture them
from a Rembrandt anatomy lesson:
that flower vase of curious heads
or attendant with a metal bowl
as I'm lain on my side, my skull
clamped to keep it still.

So the surgeons make a start
and by their skill are grown
old masters.
               Picking my brains
with suction, high-speed drill
minutely for eight whole hours
they make a work of art.

4

With a respirator's desperate wheeze
or snores and other sounds of night
an awareness of surroundings ends
in the self-concern of illness —
taking strength from other people.

Whoever that hurried nurse attends
it isn't you: her clacking feet
continue beyond your curtains.

He needs a shot of morphine.
This pain is hard enough to bear
but others' how much harder
as I wait for the oblivion
in my own breath and heartbeat.

5

Dozing off, I have vague nightmares
then, waking, find it is still dark,
part deaf and thinly muted, wait
for a nurse or through flowered curtains
faint brightenings in the sky.

Blood had oozed from one of my ears.
Half the mouth and right lid don't work.
Then drilling sounds. Heatpipes vibrate.
Although the lid irresistibly opens
iris and white stay dry.

6

At last, here comes your nurse
with a smile, a kidney bowl,
syringe of water, towel,
warm hand to soothe a retching face.

Thoroughly washed by another hand,
turned, then changed, relieved of pain
you're half a child or half a corpse?
There is pleasure and discomfort
in food and toilet training.
My whole body's to be learned again.

7

'It's quiet in here,' a cleaner says
drawing sun-filled curtains; patients
propped on beds or armchairs,
always together and always
apart, in their still elsewheres...

'It's a comedy,' one of them mumbles.
He'd been shuffling to the bathroom
but, come back for a mislaid sponge,
'a comedy routine,' he'd said
to somebody in an adjacent bed
discharged for just the weekend,
waiting to be taken home.

8

Stoic resilience in the language!
'How much can you stand?'
A paralysed pensioner
lifted on his bedside
by two nurses had been asked.
'Stand what?' he replied.

Put to shame by others' patience
I'm not one to judge.
With no music, books, or family
how do they pass the time
through a whole day's sun-struck hours
staring at a window ledge
filled with wilted peonies?

9

The calm, remorseless humour
for acquaintances and friends
or unusual sang-froid means
not scaring other people
when they come to visit you
with a thermos flask of soup,
a newspaper, cassette, or fruit,
profuse and upright flowers.

10

Head to my pillow in visiting hours
you were whispering a secret.
You'd got pregnant once and lost it?
How come I never knew?
An intravenous drip support
and suction pump to clear the throat
stood by us while you had your say
at the end of another nursed hospital day
when somebody drew the curtains.

You said it because I might be needing
reassurance of ordinary powers;
but lines about your face and eyes
had realigned at my replies'
falterings, a similar loneliness.
Like an ex-Yugoslavian port
in delicate pastel on the room's far wall,
a life that was not to be part of ours,
it beckoned, just, receding.

11

Whole packs of pastel *Get Well* cards
are pinned above recumbent heads.
Their photos of grandchildren
have been shown to fill in time.

Best wishes from near strangers:
a retired parson by the bed
who'd known my dad at college
was only the most unexpected.

There were visits from a godfather
who'd not been seen in thirty years
– how odd to recognize him
through the damage of the years.

These veterans from that post-war vote
which promised us a National Health
have paid to see it cut and cut:
why aren't they desperate?

12

Sudden rain seen against pale foliage
unfolding beyond the gymnasium window,
rain come as if to soothe this burning
darkens by degrees an asphalt pavement.
So how much would you say you're worth?

Hands firm on a wooden bar, stood tiptoe
ten times and counting, with each I glimpse
fresh green shoots taken hold this spring:
one day discovering words to be said
quietly, at intervals, is something I have
to give of this half-over life they save
for the same price as a roof above my head.

13

Listening to the accents
like sister's hidden scouse
or a Norfolk farmer's burr,
that day I heard a staff nurse
phoning round the wards for
any possible assistance.
There were her post-op patients
crying out in agonies
and others: the routine
for a Chilean auxiliary
who must have fled from Pinochet,
an Iraqi living fifteen years
in this haven, as it was,
for economic migrants
– like a puzzled Neapolitan
who'd come here all my life ago
and me, how much I owe
my country, oh my country
where they work to keep us whole.

14

An abated fever of attention round me
barely perceptibly shifts its focus
onto another's pre-operative fears,
or a young woman's punctual howls
repeated like an air-raid siren,
only release of her sorrow and rages,
'distressing everyone,' a sister says.
'Sometimes you just go home in tears.'

Become a favourite of the night shift
I hardly take up any time,
am moved to ease bed shortages
from ward to ward to visitors' room
with apologies, repeated goodbyes: had left
as if going home by gentle stages.

15

About the perimeter of eighteen holes,
within light shadow cast by trees
golfers are stooping to adjust tees
while someone else vigorously strolls

in the pink of a sunset, near this end
of a day when if not getting worse
I seem to have made little progress
and naturally grow disheartened.

Bell's palsy twice froze half your smile.
My right eye will not blink or close.
But it's no tragedy if a son grows
to look like his mother, said Oscar Wilde.

Mum, you look to me with fond eyes,
relieved a curious fate has spared
your first-born, though faintly marred,
and marred in a way you recognize.

CONVALESCENT DAYS

for the Friends

I wake as a cock crows into the haze
of Lacrilube eye-gel. My convalescence
has blurred slow, changeable summer.
Arranged rose petals imperceptibly age
on a window sill. The sloping lawn
is speckled with daisies and dark birds.

Leisurely debates about what birds
have dared to feed bring back a haze
of handbook illustrations to the lawn.
Lunching with friends helps convalescence.
Chaffinch, thrush, a starling? At my age
I ought to know. It's already late summer.

You've made a present of this summer,
its lost hamster, hurt ginger tom, the birds
taking dust-baths. Bad news in our age
of domestic wars homes through a haze
brought by too much sun. Convalescence
is no trouble. Someone mows the lawn.

In avenues and parks beyond edged lawn
life expands across distances all summer,
then shrinks to headaches of convalescence.
On a video, forgotten hits by the Byrds
start into a fiercely yearning haze
that means remorse. So this is middle age,

and we have begun to feel our age.
The shadowy figures round your lawn
are husbands and wives lost in the haze
or manoeuvrings of a different summer.
What went wrong? We're not free birds,
and life itself's become a convalescence.

Keeping going is what convalescence
mainly entails. One daughter's of an age
(or thinks so) to act like the little birds
and bees; she sunbathes, sulking on cut lawn,
plays social tennis or piano through summer.
Carol, she's your own Dolores Haze.

Most of these birds will abandon your lawn,
and convalescence is another way to age;
just so the summers must become autumnal haze.

AFTERLIVES

What returns beside Foss Island

in the small hours? Sobering shame
or blushes at faults in earlier work,
hummed love songs. Tell me, what became

of so-and-so who survived each knock
and pulled back with a purpose?
Who humiliated? Who had luck

among mentors reduced to shadows
of themselves, or shadows themselves?
A shuddering privet. Who would suppose

just this remained? The broken resolves
to mend by town walls I passed under.
What is there now the pavement shelves

for someone grown older, fonder?